NOW THAT YOU

Believe

162 BIBLE VERSES
TO LEARN & UNDERSTAND

B. AKINTOKUN

ACKNOWLEDGMENT

I would like to recognise my nearest and dearest friends and family, home and abroad, for taking their time to look through the rough drafts, creating a structure and making suggestions for corrections.

Also, to my Pastors for their encouragement and support.

DEDICATION

This book is dedicated to every new believer as the message of Christ is preached.

Every child coming to know the Gospel of our Lord.

Every believer in the Gospel of Christ.

PREFACE

Out of the mouth of babes and sucklings
hast thou ordained strength because of
thine enemies, that thou mightest still the
enemy and the avenger.

Psalm 8:2
KJV

SECTIONS

YOUR SALVATION
IS ROOTED IN YOUR
FAITH IN GOD

For by grace you have been
saved through faith. And this is
not your own doing; it is the gift
of God.

Ephesians 2:8
ESV

And without faith it is impossible
to please God, because anyone who
comes to him must believe that he
exists and that he rewards those
who earnestly seek him.

Hebrews 11:6
NIV

Now faith is the substance of
things hoped for, the evidence
of things not seen.

Hebrews 11:1
NKJV

So faith comes from hearing,
that is, hearing the Good News
about Christ.

Romans 10:17
NLT

And the prayer of faith will save the
sick, and the Lord will raise him
up. And if he has committed sins,
he will be forgiven.

James 5:15
NKJV

And the Lord said, "If you had faith like a grain of mustard seed, you could say to this mulberry tree, 'Be uprooted and planted in the sea,' and it would obey you.

Luke 17:6
ESV

By faith, we see the world called into existence by God's word, what we see created by what we don't see.

Hebrews 11:3
MSG

For in it the righteousness of God is
revealed from faith to faith; as it is
written, "The just shall live by faith."

Romans 1:17
NKJV

For we maintain that a person is
justified by faith apart from the
works of the law.

Romans 3:28
NIV

Yet we know that a person is made right with God by faith in Jesus Christ, not by obeying the law. And we have believed in Christ Jesus, so that we might be made right with God because of our faith in Christ, not because we have obeyed the law. For no one will ever be made right with God by obeying the law.

Galatians 2:16
NLT

Therefore, since we have been made
right in God's sight by faith, we have
peace with God because of what Jesus
Christ our Lord has done for us.

Romans 5:1
NLT

For the Scriptures tell us, "Abraham
believed God, and God counted him as
righteous because of his faith."

Romans 4:3
NLT

Since Jesus died and broke loose from
the grave, God will most certainly bring
back to life those who died in Jesus.

1 Thessalonians 4:14
MSG

Because of Christ and our faith in
him, we can now come boldly and
confidently into God's presence.

Ephesians 3:12
NLT

Because of our faith, Christ has brought
us into this place of undeserved privilege
where we now stand, and we confidently
and joyfully look forward to sharing
God's glory.

Romans 5:2
NLT

So in Christ Jesus you are all children of God through faith...

Galatians 3:26
NIV

...because, if you confess with your mouth
that Jesus is Lord and believe in your
heart that God raised him from the dead,
you will be saved.

Romans 10:9
ESV

For it is by believing in your heart
that you are made right with God, and
it is by openly declaring your faith
that you are saved.

Romans 10:10
NLT

Anyone who believes and is baptized
will be saved. But anyone who refuses
to believe will be condemned.

Mark 16:16
NLT

There is no judgment against anyone who believes in him. But anyone who does not believe in him has already been judged for not believing in God's one and only Son.

John 3:18
NLT

SECTION TWO

GOD COMMANDS

YOU TO LOVE

And though I have the gift of prophecy,
and understand all mysteries and all
knowledge, and though I have all faith, so
that I could remove mountains, but have
not love, I am nothing.

1 Corinthians 13:2
NKJV

Love never fails. But whether there are prophecies, they will fail; whether there are tongues, they will cease; whether there is knowledge, it will vanish away.

1 Corinthians 13:8
NKJV

Love does no harm to a neighbor.
Therefore love is the fulfillment
of the law.

Romans 13:10
NIV

22 But the fruit of the Spirit is love,
joy, peace, patience, kindness,
goodness, faithfulness,

23 gentleness, self-control; against
such things there is no law.

Galatians 5:22-23
ESV

But anyone who does not love does
not know God, for God is love.

1 John 4:8
NLT

For God so loved the world, that he gave
his only Son, that whoever believes in him
should not perish but have eternal life.

John 3:16
ESV

...who Himself bore our sins in His own body on the tree, that we, having died to sins, might live for righteousness—by whose stripes you were healed.

1 Peter 2:24
NKJV

There is no greater love than
to lay down one's life for
one's friends.

John 15:13
NLT

But God showed his great love for
us by sending Christ to die for us
while we were still sinners.

Romans 5:8
NLT

Behold what manner of love the Father has bestowed on us, that we should be called children of God! Therefore the world does not know us, because it did not know Him.

1 John 3:1
NKJV

Therefore you shall love the Lord your
God, and keep His charge, His statutes,
His judgments, and His
commandments always.

Deuteronomy 11:1
NKJV

SECTION THREE

JESUS;

YOUR SALVATION

And everyone who calls on the
name of the Lord will be saved.

Acts 2:21
NIV

I give them eternal life, and they
shall never perish; no one will
snatch them out of my hand.

John 10:28
NIV

Everyone who believes that Jesus is
the Christ has become a child of God.
And everyone who loves the Father
loves his children, too.

1 John 5:1
NLT

Here's a word you can take to heart and depend on: Jesus Christ came into the world to save sinners. I'm proof - Public Sinner Number One –

1 Timothy 1:15
MSG

9   Therefore God exalted him to the
highest place and gave him the name
that is above every name,

10   that at the name of Jesus every
knee should bow, in heaven and on
earth and under the earth,

11   and every tongue acknowledge
that Jesus Christ is Lord, to the glory
of God the Father.

Philippians 2:9-11
NIV

...and by Him everyone who
believes is justified from all
things from which you could not
be justified by the law of Moses.

Acts 13:39
NKJV

Yet to all who did receive him, to those who believed in his name, he gave the right to become children of God—

John 1:12
NIV

And they overcame him by the blood
of the Lamb and by the word of their
testimony, and they did not love their
lives to the death.

Revelation 12:11
NKJV

The Spirit of God, who raised Jesus from the dead, lives in you. And just as God raised Christ Jesus from the dead, he will give life to your mortal bodies by this same Spirit living within you.

Romans 8:11
NLT

For I am not ashamed of the gospel of Christ, for it is the power of God to salvation for everyone who believes, for the Jew first and also for the Greek.

Romans 1:16
NKJV

JESUS SAYS
OF HIMSELF

25 Jesus said to her, "I am the
resurrection and the life. The one who
believes in me will live, even though
they die;

26 and whoever lives by believing in
me will never die. Do you believe this?"

John 11:25-26
NIV

I am Light that has come into the
world so that all who believe in
me won't have to stay any longer
in the dark.

John 12:46
MSG

Truly, truly, I say to you, whoever hears my word and believes him who sent me has eternal life. He does not come into judgment, but has passed from death to life.

John 5:24
ESV

Jesus said to him, "If you can
believe, all things are possible to
him who believes."

Mark 9:23
NKJV

Every person the Father gives me
eventually comes running to me. And
once that person is with me, I hold on
and don't let go.

John 6:37
MSG

I tell you the truth, anyone who believes
in me will do the same works I have
done, and even greater works, because I
am going to be with the Father.

John 14:12
NLT

Then Jesus spoke to them again, saying, "I am the light of the world. He who follows Me shall not walk in darkness, but have the light of life."

John 8:12
NKJV

GOD EXPECTS YOU

TO LIVE AND

GROW IN FAITH

6   So then, just as you received Christ Jesus as Lord, continue to live your lives in him,

7   rooted and built up in him, strengthened in the faith as you were taught, and overflowing with thankfulness.

Colossians 2:6-7
NIV

Like newborn babies, you must crave
pure spiritual milk so that you will grow
into a full experience of salvation. Cry
out for this nourishment...

1 Peter 2:2
NLT

Then Christ will make his home in your hearts as you trust in him. Your roots will grow down into God's love and keep you strong.

Ephesians 3:17
NLT

Let the message of Christ dwell among you richly as you teach and admonish one another with all wisdom through psalms, hymns, and songs from the Spirit, singing to God with gratitude in your hearts.

Colossians 3:16
NIV

Likewise the Spirit helps us in our weakness. For we do not know what to pray for as we ought, but the Spirit himself intercedes for us with groanings too deep for words.

Romans 8:26
ESV

YOU MUST BE
WATCHFUL AS A
BELIEVER

13   Therefore take up the whole armor of God, that you may be able to withstand in the evil day, and having done all, to stand firm.

14   Stand therefore, having fastened on the belt of truth, and having put on the breastplate of righteousness,

15   and, as shoes for your feet, having put on the readiness given by the gospel of peace.

16   In all circumstances take up the shield of faith, with which you can extinguish all the flaming darts of the evil one;

17   and take the helmet of salvation, and the sword of the Spirit, which is the word of God,

18   praying at all times in the Spirit, with all prayer and supplication. To that end, keep alert with all perseverance, making supplication for all the saints,

Ephesians 6:13-18
ESV

I say this because many deceivers have gone out into the world. They deny that Jesus Christ came in a real body. Such a person is a deceiver and an antichrist.

2 John 1:7
NLT

If anyone comes to your meeting and does
not teach the truth about Christ, don't
invite that person into your home or give
any kind of encouragement.

2 John 1:10
NLT

Only be very careful to observe the commandment and the law that Moses the servant of the Lord commanded you, to love the Lord your God, and to walk in all his ways and to keep his commandments and to cling to him and to serve him with all your heart and with all your soul.

Joshua 22:5
ESV

SECTION SEVEN

———

IN GOD YOU HAVE

PROTECTION

He who dwells in the secret place of
the Most High Shall abide under the
shadow of the Almighty.

Psalm 91:1
NKJV

In peace I will lie down and
sleep, for you alone, Lord, make
me dwell in safety.

Psalm 4:8
NIV

Behold, I am the Lord, the
God of all flesh. Is there
anything too hard for Me?

Jeremiah 32:27
NKJV

11 For he will order his angels to
protect you wherever you go.

12 They will hold you up with their
hands so you won't even hurt your
foot on a stone.

*Psalm 91:11-12
NLT*

17 "These are some of the signs that will accompany believers: They will throw out demons in my name, they will speak in new tongues,

18 they will take snakes in their hands, they will drink poison and not be hurt, they will lay hands on the sick and make them well."

Mark 16:17-18
MSG

DOING GOD'S
WORK

And then he told them, Go into
all the world and preach the
Good News to everyone.

Mark 16:15
NLT

11   For the grace of God has appeared that offers salvation to all people.

12   It teaches us to say "No" to ungodliness and worldly passions, and to live self-controlled, upright and godly lives in this present age,

Titus 2:11-12
NIV

And now, Israel, what does the Lord your God ask of you but to fear the Lord your God, to walk in obedience to him, to love him, to serve the Lord your God with all your heart and with all your soul,

Deuteronomy 10:12
NIV

For we are God's handiwork, created in Christ Jesus to do good works, which God prepared in advance for us to do.

Ephesians 2:10
NIV

And whatever you do or say, do it as a representative of the Lord Jesus, giving thanks through him to God the Father.

Colossians 3:17
NLT

...being confident of this, that he who
began a good work in you will carry it
on to completion until the day of
Christ Jesus.

Philippians 1:6
NIV

God is not unjust; he will not forget your
work and the love you have shown him
as you have helped his people and
continue to help them.

Hebrews 6:10
NIV

For God has not given us a spirit
of fear, but of power and of love
and of a sound mind.

2 Timothy 1:7
NKJV

My dear children, you come from God
and belong to God. You have already won
a big victory over those false teachers, for
the Spirit in you is far stronger than
anything in the world.

1 John 4:4
MSG

Don't copy the behaviour and customs
of this world, but let God transform
you into a new person by changing the
way you think. Then you will learn to
know God's will for you, which is good
and pleasing and perfect.

Romans 12:2
NLT

5   Trust in the Lord with all your
heart, And lean not on your own
understanding;

6   In all your ways acknowledge Him,
And He shall direct your paths.

Proverbs 3:5-6
NKJV

...but the people who know their
God shall be strong, and carry
out great exploits.

Daniel 11:32
NKJV

And we know that all things work
together for good to those who love
God, to those who are the called
according to His purpose.

Romans 8:28
NKJV

For this reason I also suffer these
things; nevertheless I am not
ashamed, for I know whom I have
believed and am persuaded that He is
able to keep what I have committed to
Him until that Day.

2 Timothy 1:12
NKJV

My dear friends, don't believe everything you hear. Carefully weigh and examine what people tell you. Not everyone who talks about God comes from God. There are a lot of lying preachers loose in the world.

1 John 4:1
MSG

May the God of hope fill you with all
joy and peace as you trust in him, so
that you may overflow with hope by
the power of the Holy Spirit.

Romans 15:13
NIV

For we through the Spirit
eagerly wait for the hope of
righteousness by faith.

Galatians 5:5
NKJV

Anyone who wanders away from this
teaching has no relationship with God.
But anyone who remains in the
teaching of Christ has a relationship
with both the Father and the Son.

2 John 1:9
NLT

CHRISTIAN
CONDUCT

But seek first the kingdom of God and
his righteousness, and all these things
will be added to you.

Matthew 6:33
ESV

I have told you all this so that you
may have peace in me. Here on
earth you will have many trials and
sorrows. But take heart, because I
have overcome the world.

John 16:33
NLT

And let the peace that comes from Christ rule in your hearts. For as members of one body you are called to live in peace. And always be thankful.

Colossians 3:15
NLT

That is true. They were broken off
because of their unbelief, but you stand
fast through faith. So do not become
proud, but fear.

Romans 11:20
ESV

In the same way, faith by itself,

if it is not accompanied by

action, is dead.

James 2:17
NIV

1   I write this, dear children, to guide you
out of sin. But if anyone does sin, we have a
Priest-Friend in the presence of the Father:
Jesus Christ, righteous Jesus.

2   When he served as a sacrifice for our
sins, he solved the sin problem for
good—not only ours, but the whole world's.

1 John 2:1-2
MSG

I have stored up your word in
my heart, that I might not sin
against you.

Psalm 119:11
ESV

13 Let no one say when he is tempted, "I am being tempted by God," for God cannot be tempted with evil, and he himself tempts no one.

14 But each person is tempted when he is lured and enticed by his own desire.

James 1:13-14
ESV

Keep your eyes on Jesus, who both began and finished this race we're in. Study how he did it. Because he never lost sight of where he was headed—that exhilarating finish in and with God—he could put up with anything along the way: Cross, shame, whatever. And now he's there, in the place of honor, right alongside God.

Hebrews 12:2
MSG

Blessed is the man who remains steadfast under trial, for when he has stood the test he will receive the crown of life, which God has promised to those who love him.

James 1:12
ESV

God is faithful, who has called

you into fellowship with his Son,

Jesus Christ our Lord.

1 Corinthians 1:9
NIV

You shall love the Lord your God
with all your heart and with all
your soul and with all your might.

Deuteronomy 6:5
ESV

Look to yourselves, that we do not lose
those things we worked for, but that we
may receive a full reward.

2 John 1:8
NKJV

See that no one repays anyone evil for
evil, but always seek to do good to one
another and to everyone.

1 Thessalonians 5:15
ESV

Since you call on a Father who judges
each person's work impartially, live out
your time as foreigners here in
reverent fear.

1 Peter 1:17
NIV

Don't let anyone look down on you
because you are young, but set an example
for the believers in speech, in conduct, in
love, in faith and in purity.

1 Timothy 4:12
NIV

...not avoiding worshiping together as some do but spurring each other on, especially as we see the big Day approaching.

Hebrews 10:25
MSG

The person who wins out over the world's ways is simply the one who believes Jesus is the Son of God.

1 John 5:5
MSG

These things I have written to you who believe in the name of the Son of God, that you may know that you have eternal life, and that you may continue to believe in the name of the Son of God.

1 John 5:13
NKJV

1   Therefore be imitators of God as
dear children.

2   And walk in love, as Christ also has
loved us and given Himself for us, an
offering and a sacrifice to God for a
sweet-smelling aroma.

Ephesians 5:1-2
NKJV

The Lord your God is with you, the Mighty Warrior who saves. He will take great delight in you; in his love he will no longer rebuke you, but will rejoice over you with singing.

Zephaniah 3:17
NIV

A new commandment I give to you, that you love one another: just as I have loved you, you also are to love one another

John 13:34
ESV

If you love me, keep my commands.

John 14:15
NIV

This is how everyone will recognize that
you are my disciples - when they see the
love you have for each other.

John 13:35
MSG

Don't love the world's ways. Don't love the world's goods. Love of the world squeezes out love for the Father.

1 John 2:15
MSG

Finally, all of you, have unity of mind,
sympathy, brotherly love, a tender heart,
and a humble mind.

1 Peter 3:8
ESV

SECTION TEN

YOU HAVE

COMFORT IN GOD

Why, my soul, are you downcast?
Why so disturbed within me? Put
your hope in God, for I will yet praise
him, my Savior and my God.

Psalm 43:5
NIV

Scripture reassures us, "No one who
trusts God like this - heart and soul -
will ever regret it."

Romans 10:11
MSG

A single day in your courts is better
than a thousand anywhere else! I would
rather be a gatekeeper in the house of
my God than live the good life in the
homes of the wicked.

Psalm 84:10
NLT

One thing I have desired of the Lord,
That will I seek: That I may dwell in the
house of the Lord All the days of my
life, To behold the beauty of the Lord,
And to inquire in His temple.

Psalm 27:4
NKJV

I will never forget your
precepts, for by them you
have preserved my life.

Psalm 119:93
NIV

When doubts filled my mind,
your comfort gave me renewed
hope and cheer.

Psalm 94:19
NLT

Know therefore that the Lord your God is God; he is the faithful God, keeping his covenant of love to a thousand generations of those who love him and keep his commandments.

Deuteronomy 7:9
NIV

If any of you lacks wisdom, let him ask God,
who gives generously to all without
reproach, and it will be given him.

James 1:5
ESV

Therefore I tell you, whatever you ask
for in prayer, believe that you have
received it, and it will be yours.

Mark 11:24
NIV

And all the believers lived in a
wonderful harmony, holding
everything in common.

Acts 2:44
MSG

And since we died with Christ, we
know we will also live with him

Romans 6:8
NLT

7   My victory and honor come from God alone. He is my refuge, a rock where no enemy can reach me.

8   O my people, trust in him at all times. Pour out your heart to him, for God is our refuge.

Psalm 62:7-8
NLT

How great are His signs, And how mighty
His wonders! His kingdom is an
everlasting kingdom, And His dominion
is from generation to generation.

Daniel 4:3
NKJV

Who shall separate us from the love of Christ? Shall trouble or hardship or persecution or famine or nakedness or danger or sword?

Romans 8:35
NIV

No, in all these things we are
more than conquerors through
him who loved us.

Romans 8:37
ESV

No power in the sky above or in the earth below— indeed, nothing in all creation will ever be able to separate us from the love of God that is revealed in Christ Jesus our Lord.

Romans 8:39
NLT

For in this hope we were saved. Now hope that is seen is not hope. For who hopes for what he sees?

Romans 8:24
ESV

Now hope does not disappoint,
because the love of God has been
poured out in our hearts by the
Holy Spirit who was given to us.

Romans 5:5
NKJV

Be joyful in hope, patient in
affliction, faithful in prayer.

Romans 12:12
NIV

Rejoice in the Lord always.

Again I will say, rejoice!

Philippians 4:4
NKJV

FAITH

CONFESSIONS

The lines have fallen to me in pleasant places; Yes, I have a good inheritance.

Psalm 16:6
NKJV

I have been crucified with Christ; it is no longer I who live, but Christ lives in me; and the life which I now live in the flesh I live by faith in the Son of God, who loved me and gave Himself for me.

Galatians 2:20
NKJV

Yea, though I walk through the valley
of the shadow of death, I will fear no
evil; For You are with me; Your rod and
Your staff, they comfort me.

Psalm 23:4
NKJV

You are my hiding place; you will
protect me from trouble and surround
me with songs of deliverance.

Psalm 32:7
NIV

The LORD is my light and my
salvation— so why should I be afraid?
The LORD is my fortress, protecting
me from danger, so why should I
tremble?

Psalm 27:1
NLT

I'll tell the world how great and
good you are, I'll shout Hallelujah
all day, every day.

Psalm 35:28
MSG

I can do all things through Christ
who strengthens me.

Philippians 4:13
NKJV

The LORD is my shepherd;
I have all that I need.

Psalm 23:1
NLT

... I am like an olive tree, thriving in
the house of God. I will always trust in
God's unfailing love.

Psalm 52:8
NLT

I will praise the Lord, who
counsels me; even at night my
heart instructs me.

Psalm 16:7
NIV

I will say of the Lord, "He is my
refuge and my fortress; My God,
in Him I will trust."

Psalm 91:2
NKJV

For in the day of trouble he will keep me
safe in his dwelling; he will hide me in
the shelter of his sacred tent and set me
high upon a rock.

Psalm 27:5
NIV

...as for me and my house, we will
serve the LORD.

Joshua 24:15
ESV

Surely goodness and mercy shall
follow me all the days of my life, and
I shall dwell in the house of the
LORD forever.

Psalm 23:6
ESV

SECTION TWELVE

YOU HAVE HOPE

IN ETERNAL LIFE

13   And now, dear brothers and sisters, we want you to know what will happen to the believers who have died so you will not grieve like people who have no hope.

14   For since we believe that Jesus died and rose again, even so, through Jesus, God will bring with him those who have fallen asleep.

1 Thessalonians 4:13-14
NLT

This truth gives them confidence that
they have eternal life, which
God—who does not lie—promised
them before the world began.

Titus 1:2
NLT

Because of his grace he made us right
in his sight and gave us confidence
that we will inherit eternal life.

Titus 3:7
NLT

Printed in Poland
by Amazon Fulfillment
Poland Sp. z o.o., Wrocław
13 March 2022